SAVING FOR SCHOOL

Also by Gail Vaz-Oxlade

Money Rules
Money-Smart Kids
It's Your Money
Never Too Late
Debt-Free Forever

SAVING
FOR
SCHOOL

Understand RESPs, Take Control of Your
Savings, Minimize Student Debt

Gail Vaz-Oxlade

Collins

Published by Collins, an imprint of HarperCollins Publishers Ltd

First edition

HarperCollins Publishers Ltd
2 Bloor Street East, 20th Floor
Toronto, Ontario, Canada
M4W 1A8

www.harpercollins.ca

Library and Archives Canada Cataloguing in Publication information
is available upon request

ISBN 978-1-44341-868-3

Printed and bound in Canada
WEB 9 8 7 6 5 4 3 2 1

To the young 'uns in my life who listened carefully.
I'm honoured to have been able to guide you.
I love you all tremendously and am so proud of how
nicely you've grown up.

CONTENTS

....

Introduction

· · · · · · · · · · · · · · · · · · · ·

I'm not sure why it is that so many people refuse to take free money. "Free" isn't often really free, and when it is, we should be leaping at the opportunity. Maybe you just don't know that the government wants to GIVE you money for your child's future education. Maybe you don't believe that "free" is really free. Or maybe you're so unsure of how to get the free money, you've yet to take action. Let me assure you that a Registered Education Savings Plan (RESP) is a fabulous way to save for school. And, yes, you get free money if you follow the rules. So please, please, do not turn your back on this opportunity to help your son or daughter. Opportunities like this are few and far between and this is your chance to take full advantage of "free."

It seems like a lifetime ago that my children were born. I was 34 when I had Alexandra and almost 37 when

Malcolm came along. My children changed everything about my life: where I lived, how I worked, when I worked, what I did with my "spare time." Ha! Spare time was a thing of the past, as was spare money.

Being self-employed meant that when I went on maternity leave, there was no money from the employment insurance system. I had to have a stash of cash in the bank to take care of my share of the household bills. But even though there wasn't much money to spare, as soon as Alex was born, I started putting money away for her post-secondary education. I'd seen the stats about what it would cost; it turned out they underestimated.

There are three ways to pay for post-secondary education: (1) save the money while the kids are young, (2) come up with the money each year as your child goes through school, and (3) borrow.

Since I'm of a savings mind and was strongly committed to ensuring the funds were available should my kids decide to pursue a higher education, I saved. Alex's undergrad degree cost about $18,000 a year—that's $72,000 for a four-year degree. Half of that was tuition. The rest went to books, lab fees, housing, utilities, Internet, food, transportation, clothes and the like.

Lest you think that Alex lived a high-style life while at university, let me describe the house she shared. Imagine a regular-sized two-bedroom home with a sunroom and a finished basement. Sounds nice, doesn't it? Now imagine that every single room in the house—except the two kitchens and two bathrooms—has been turned into a bedroom. Alex had six roommates in that small two-bedroom house. Seven kids shared two bathrooms and two kitchens. We're not talking cushy here.

Had I used the RESP money alone to see Alex through her undergrad, we would have blown through all the money before the end of year three. I wanted to be sure she didn't graduate with an albatross of debt around her neck. That's a hell of a way to start a life. So I paid for her housing expenses out of my cash flow and used her RESP for all things school-related, like tuition and books.

Coming up with the money from cash flow doesn't have to all fall on a parent's shoulders. Kids have a role to play in picking up a part of the tab for their own education. But there are some programs that are so intensive that working while in school is impossible. And of late, the summer job landscape has been bleak. So university and college students are taking on debt at a wicked clip to complete their degrees.

While student debt is considered "good" debt, that only holds true if you don't take on too much and can pay it back quickly. Many people are unaware that the default student-loan minimum payment will keep a body in debt for almost 10 years. And since the interest rate on student loans is no great deal—it's actually higher than what you'd pay to a regular lender to offset the interest-free period while students are in school—that default minimum can mean huge interest costs.

Graduates are coming out of school with record levels of debt. According to the Canadian Federation of Students, the average debt for university graduates is almost $27,000. Lest you think that doesn't sound like so much, let me point out that's an average. Since there are many kids graduating without any debt at all, because their parents had the fore-sight to save and could afford to help, those who do have debt have far more debt than the average would indicate. Did you know that the Canada Student Loans Program is close to hitting its $15-billion threshold years in advance? That's a direct result of the fact that the cost of getting an education has gone up disproportionately to inflation. And the trend shows no sign of reversing.

It doesn't take a huge amount of money to make a dif-ference if you put enough time on your side. I started with $100 a month. Every month, I had that amount debited from my chequing account and moved over to an account for Alex. When Malcolm came along, I did exactly the same thing. And the counter just ticked along, month after month.

When I first opened post-secondary savings accounts for my children, I did not use the RESP. At the time, the restrictions on what the money could be used for were much tighter than those of today's RESPs. Group RESPs were much more popular than bank-run RESPs, and I didn't want to get stuck in a system that provided so little flexibility. What if I had a tough month or two? What if one of the kids decided not to go further than high school?

4

I wasn't prepared to forgo my hard-earned money. And I hate penalties and fees!

When the legislation changed and RESPs became the fabulous education savings plans they are now, I jumped on them. I had years of catching up to do and I got busy.

One of the things that made the new-and-improved RESP so attractive was the introduction of the Canada Education Savings Grant (CESG). This is FREE MONEY that the government gives to families as an incentive to save for their children's future education. When you put $100 into an RESP for an eligible child, the government gives you $20. That's right, GIVES you. That's like getting 20% interest on your money without having to do a thing. It boggles my mind that every single parent doesn't have an RESP for each of their children. Who turns their back on free money?

More than half of Canadians do. Lord love a duck! As of the end of 2010 (the last year for which Statistics Canada published numbers), less than 43% of those children who were eligible for the CESG were getting it.

Parents, you can't complain about how much school is costing your kids, how much debt your children will graduate with or how hard it is to find money to save if you're prepared to turn your back on free money. No one says you have to start by maxing out the RESP every year. I didn't. On a maternity leave budget with very little cash to spare, all I could come up with was $100 a month. If you can only swing $50, so be it. That works out to about $1.67

a day, or one cup of not-very-expensive drive-through coffee. Is your child's future worth $1.67 to you?

You can plan now or pay later. Or you can do nothing and hope your children can work their way through university or get good enough jobs to get their debt paid off lickety-split. School costs are only going to keep going up.

When Alex was a baby, the projected cost for her four-year degree was $42,000. That number is burned in my memory because I so vividly remember thinking, "How the hell am I going to get to $42,000 in savings?" Turns out, the projections were on the low side, but the magic of compounding return did its job. I got to the $42,000 plus some with diligent savings and good returns on my investments.

Today's projections are enough to scare your pants off! It's been estimated that the cost of a four-year degree will be between $100,000 and $140,000 in 18 years, depending on whether a student lives at home or is submersed in the university experience. Given that Alex's annual cost in 2012 was $18,000 to live away from home, I totally buy the projections.

Thank heavens I'm a planner and had the foresight to start saving for the children's schooling as soon as they were born. I set aside $100 a month and, lest you think that $100 each and every month was a lot, let me tell you how it shook out in the end. While Alex was in school, it cost $800 a month in tuition for her undergrad degree. That did not include the money I forked out to keep her sheltered and clothed. All told, her schooling costs were about $1,500 a month. That would have put a serious crimp in the rest of my spending if I hadn't had the stash of cash I'd saved little by little.

I've heard parents say things like, "I had to pay my way through school," and "If he wants an education he'll have to find a way to pay for it." Hey, back then, tuitions were lower—much lower—as was the cost of living. You could earn enough by working through the summer to have your tuition, if not your total year's expenses, in hand before you had to go back to school. Find me a job now where kids can earn $18,000 in the four months they're out of school each year, if they can find a job at all!

If you don't much care whether your kid gets an education or not, don't even bother to read this book. But if you're the parent who wants to do whatever it takes to help, I'm going to show you how to make what you save work as hard as possible to give your kids the opportunities you want them to have.

My big message is simple: if you have a child under the age of 15, open up an RESP today. It doesn't matter how little money you save; whatever you put away is debt your Darling Daughter or Sweet Son won't have to shoulder later. AND YOU'LL GET (at least some of) THE FREE MONEY!

ONE

How to Save
. . . .

So you're convinced you have to do something to help Sonny and Darling come up with the money for school. Your next question is, "Where am I going to find the money?"

FIND THE MONEY

Ever since David Bach coined the phrase "Latte Factor" to describe how much money we waste that we could be saving instead, morning coffee has been under assault. Sometimes it feels like we're not allowed to spend anything on simple pleasures because we must save more! It can be very frustrating.

Saving is a choice. Just as buying a new pair of shoes, a magazine or a cuppa java in the morning is a choice, so too is saving. You don't have to do it to the exclusion of everything else you enjoy in your life. But if saving for your child's future is something that's important to you, then you'll have to look for ways to spend less so that you have the money to squirrel away.

People hate to not spend money. Spending is so much more fun. Hey, my eyes light up when I see a great deal on skeins of yarn or a new book I'd like to read. But if, as parents, we've decided to save for our little one's future, then find the money we must. You might be surprised at all the ways you can come up with $10 here and $5 there to make an RESP contribution big enough to grab all the grant money to which Sonny and Darling are entitled.

Find $2 a Day

• Unplug appliances like TVs, DVD players, cellphone chargers and computers when not in use. According to Energy Star, 75% of the electricity used over the lifetime of home electronics is consumed when the products are turned OFF. We've even coined a term for the use of electricity when an appliance is off: "phantom load."
• Instead of buying or renting movies, borrow them from your local library. They are FREE.
• Once you've got your emergency fund in place, raise the deductibles on your car and home insurance. You wouldn't make a claim for under $1,000 (if you did, you would soon find your insurance costs in the stratosphere), so why have a $250 or $500 deductible?

- Switch to a no-fee bank account and a no-fee credit card.
- Hang your clothes to dry and turn off the dryer cycle on your dishwasher.
- Buy in bulk with friends and split the savings.
- Like to hit the fast-food outlets or drive-through windows? Keep a tin in your car and every time you pick up a coffee, grab a sub or munch on a muffin, drop a buck in your tin. This is your Fast-Food Tax. Hey, if you can find the money for the drive-through, you can find the money to save for your kids' futures too!
- Eliminate your paper bills and the typical $2 fee that comes with them.
- Swap convenience for savings. Pay your house and car insurance in one lump sum and save about $100 in interest charges. (Yes, they charge interest if you pay in instalments.)
- Downgrade your personal cellphone usage and costs.

Find $5 a Day

- Cut out the newspaper and morning coffee purchase. Brew at home and chip in with friends to buy one newspaper between three or four of you and save the difference.
- Bag your lunch. Cook enough dinner the night before to take leftovers to work for lunch. Take the ingredients for a delicious sandwich to work and assemble it fresh. Make a huge pot of soup, stew or chili, freeze it in single servings and cart it to work, where you can warm it up and enjoy it along with crusty bread or a salad.

- Shop at second-hand and consignment stores. Kids outgrow their clothes faster than they can wear them out. And new to you is a good alternative to brand spanking new. You'll pay half or less of what you would at full retail.
- Switch to water. Eliminate the diet pop, juices and other beverages you typically buy, and for heaven's sake, stop buying bottled water!
- Skip prepared foods and cook from scratch. Yes, you'll have to cut your own veggies and fruit, skin and debone your chicken, and peel your own potatoes to make fries, but you'll save a whack of money.
- Save your "savings." If you save $5 by shopping the sales, by using coupons or just by being a smart shopper, take that $5 and stick it in your Savings container at home. If you don't, you'll just spend it somewhere else and then you won't have saved a penny. Some financial institutions, like ING Direct, have an app where you can put in how much you have saved on a purchase and it will automatically transfer that amount from your chequing account to your savings, all via your smart phone.

Find $10 a Day

- Carpool. Use public transit. Ride your bike. Walk. 'Nuff said.
- Move your savings to a high-interest savings account that pays at least 1.5% interest on your balance.
- Eliminate one extracurricular activity a week from your child's schedule. We have a tendency to over-program for

our kids. Help them learn to be their own best friend and entertain themselves by reading, doing arts and crafts or riding their bikes through the neighbourhood. Solo play gives kids time to think and use their imagination.

• Lose the expensive bad habits. The stats say that Canadians spend about 2% of their income on alcohol and tobacco. You can't tell me you don't have money to save if you're watching your money go up in smoke or down the potty.

• Use students for services ranging from hair to tooth care to save money. Check out local schools of cosmetology, dentistry, massage and the like.

• Swap eating out in restaurants for potluck dinners with friends.

• Save your extra paycheque. Set up your budget to accommodate two or four paycheques a month, depending on your pay schedule. Some months you may get an extra cheque, and that can be a boon to your educational savings.

• Go over your bills and see where you may be spending money for a service you don't really benefit from. Are you paying to have movies piped in to your TV that you never seem to watch? Axe it. Paying for a membership at a gym that you haven't visited in six months? Lose it. Spending even $1 in banking machine fees? Cut it out! Look for all the things you pay for but seldom use, and as you chop, trim, slice and dice, make a list of the money you're saving.

• Get enough individual term insurance and drop the creditor and mortgage life insurance premiums from your credit cards and mortgage.

Get Friends and Family In on the Savings

Most of us have ways we can trim our spending to find the money for something that's really, really important to us. All you have to decide now is whether saving for your child's future is more or less important than spending money in some other way. Get creative and you can find ways to save if that's a priority.

But trimming isn't the only way to come up with money for an RESP. Get your family and friends involved. If having money for school is important, ask that as an alternative to tons of pressies on birthdays and other special days, family and friends give a small gift and a contribution to the RESP. It's amazing how those $20 contributions add up over time.

You should maintain control over the actual opening of and contributing to an RESP if friends and family are going to help, and I'll explain why in detail later. For now, just know that it's a good idea to have one plan and for you to be the conduit for contributions to that plan as the subscriber.

Get Your Kids In on the Savings

The only exception to the one-plan rule is if kids are going to be making contributions to their own RESPs themselves. Since you can open an RESP at any age, Darling can open one for herself, make the contributions from her own resources and get the grant money she's entitled to for having a plan. Since any contributions she makes remain hers and can be taken out without any tax consequences, Darling should have her own plan so that her hard-earned bucks stay in her pocket.

Not all parents have the resources to maximize RESP contributions to get all the grant money available to a child. If Darling wants to save a portion of her earnings for school from summer work, a part-time job or a small business she's created for herself, and there is still grant money available to be claimed, she should use an RESP to get as much of that money as she can.

When kids are old enough to earn money of their own, have a discussion about how they will contribute to their own educational savings. Will they sock away 20% of every dollar earned for school? Or will it be closer to 40%? How much they contribute is a good place to start the discussion about students taking responsibility for their own education.

There are many stories of kids who get a free ride through college or university and take six years to get a four-year degree because (a) they spend too much time partying to pass or (b) they keep changing their minds. While it's unrealistic to think all young people go into post-secondary education with their future goals locked and loaded, there are consequences for switching programs and taking more than the normal amount of time to finish up.

When Alex went to university, it was with the under-standing that she would be responsible for one-third of her costs. The same deal holds for Malcolm. I wanted them to have a financial stake in the experience. Since neither would qualify for student loans because of my income, I needed some way of putting the ball in their court.

Alex discontinued her education after three years. Yup, she dropped out! University wasn't for her. She has decided to try another path for now. I encouraged her to live a life true to her own desires and beliefs. I told her that she was off the ticket, that I'd help her with first and last months' rent. I also told her the money would still be there down the road if she decided to go back to school.

I have two wishes for my children: that they can take care of themselves and that they are happy. Part of being able to take care of themselves is being financially self-reliant. Part of being happy is being self-determining. They have to figure out how to balance the two.

FIND THE PLAN

So you're convinced you're going to have to come up with some money to save for your kids' futures. And you're convinced that getting the free money that comes with an RESP is a good idea. Well, it's a good idea if you can just figure out how the damn things work. There seem to be so many rules, so many acronyms, so many "ifs" and "thens." You're right. It's a bloody nightmare trying to piece out how RESPs operate. Sometimes some of the rules make ME scratch my head. But if you want to save for your child's education, an RESP is the best way to do it, so figure it out you must.

Why am I so sure RESPs are the way to go? One word: CESG. It's not actually a word; it's an acronym that stands for Canada Education Savings Grant. I'm just going to call it the "Grant Money" for the sake of ease. You'll want to pay attention because it's not often the government *gives you* money.

Here's how an RESP works. You open up a plan, so you're the "plan owner" or "subscriber." You deposit some money for your kid, who is the "beneficiary." The government matches your deposit, giving you 20 cents for every dollar you contribute up to an annual maximum. That's the Grant Money. The money you deposit and the Grant Money can both be invested to earn a return. You might use a savings account, a Guaranteed Investment Certificate (GIC), a mutual fund, a bond, a stock or some other investment option to make that money grow. Whatever you choose to invest in, the income you earn inside the RESP grows on a tax-deferred basis, so the income—be it interest, dividends or capital gains—inside the RESP is not taxed as long as it is in the plan. That means it can compound faster to make more money until it's time to take the money out to send the kids off to school. At that point, any income earned in the plan is taxed in your child's hands as it is withdrawn. There's no tax payable on the original deposit or on the Grant Money. But the income you earned on both in the plan will be taxed.

You put money in. The government puts money in. The whole shebang is invested and grows tax-deferred, and when it comes time for post-secondary school, Sonny and Darling have a pool of money to minimize the amount of debt they must take on to get an education. Sweet!

DOES YOUR CHILD QUALIFY?

To be eligible as a beneficiary of an RESP, your child must be a resident of Canada and 17 years of age or younger by the end of the calendar year in which you wish to make a contribution. So if Sonny is turning 17 this year, this is the last year for which you'll be able to make a contribution for him, and it needs to be in by December 31.

There are special rules in place for children who are 16 or 17. They can only qualify for Grant Money if:

(a) At least a total of $2,000 was contributed to the RESP and not withdrawn from any RESP for Sonny before the end of the calendar year in which he turned 15, or

(b) At least $100 was contributed and not withdrawn for each of the four years prior to the end of the calendar year in which he turned 15 (so you would have to have made at least a $100 contribution when Sonny was 12, 13, 14 and 15 to stay on the right side of this rule)

These two rules mean that if you want to get any Grant Money at all, the last year you can wait to open an RESP for Sonny is the year he turns 15 (so long as you have a full $2,000 to contribute). So if Sonny turns 15 in January, you still have until December to make the contribution. Wait later than that and you'll forgo all the Grant Money that was available, so the RESP may no longer be the best option.

GATHER YOUR DOCUMENTATION

Once you've determined that Darling qualifies, it's time to gather the paperwork you're going to need to open up a plan.

You will need to have a social insurance number (SIN) as the "subscriber" to the plan—or the person who makes the contributions. You will also need a SIN for your child as the "beneficiary" of the plan—or the person who uses the money.

GAIL'S TIP

Subscribers can change under specific circumstances. The two circumstances under which the RESP subscriber can be changed are:

(a) If there is a divorce and one spouse acquires the subscriber's rights under the dissolution agreement, and

(b) If the original subscriber dies; the deceased's estate may become the subscriber or an alternate-named subscriber may take over

Warning: Anyone who acquires your rights as the subscriber will become the de facto owner of the plan, as if that person made all the contributions. The money doesn't actually belong to your child until payments start coming out of the RESP; up to that point, the money belongs to the subscriber.

So if you name your sister as your replacement under your will, all the money contributed to the RESP becomes her money to do with as she wishes (she could withdraw it early or keep it in place for your child). You better be able to trust your replacement subscriber with the money you've saved up for Darling's schooling.

If you haven't named a replacement subscriber, the next person to make a contribution to the RESP becomes the subscriber. Yup, you heard me right. Anyone who makes the next contribution to the RESP automatically becomes the subscriber. So if your ex-husband is the first person to put more money into the plan, all the money within the plan becomes his money until it is paid out to your child. If he chooses to withdraw the amounts contributed, he may do so at any time.

If you already have an RESP and you haven't made a provision in your will for who gets to be in charge of it, today's the day to do it!

....

Only parents or legal guardians can apply for a SIN for a child under 12. Children who are 12 or older can apply for their own SINs.

You can apply for your child's SIN in person at your nearest Service Canada centre. As long as you have all the right documentation, including:

• a birth certificate issued by the province or territory where the child was born, or
• a Canadian citizenship certificate issued by Citizenship and Immigration Canada

you'll get the number on your first visit and receive the SIN card in the mail. If you want to apply by mail, there's an application form on Service Canada's website that you can complete and mail in. However, you have to provide original documents, so make sure you send them in a way that keeps them safe and guarantees their arrival.

For newborns, you can use the Newborn Registration Service available in many provinces to apply for his or her SIN when you register your child's birth. There is no fee for applying for a SIN.

CHOOSE A PLAN PROVIDER

One of the first questions most people have when they decide to open up an RESP for their wee one is, "Where?" You could do it at your bank, or at some other company that sells RESPs, as long as you've done your homework and are getting the support and service you need to see your way through the process.

Most people choose to hold their RESPs at the same place they have their bank accounts, RRSPs or some other financial product or service, drawing on the relationship they already have to guide them through the process. Since individual and family RESPs can be moved to another provider should the relationship prove to be less than satisfactory down the road, this is a fine place to start.

Ask These Three Questions

The first question you're going to ask is, **"Is your plan an individual, family or group plan?"**

If the RESP is a group plan, steer clear. I'll talk more about individual and family plans shortly. For now, just eliminate the group RESPs from your list of potential providers.

I am not a fan of group RESPs, which are sometimes called "scholarship trusts." While these plans make up about 30% of the market and have brochures prominently displayed in hospitals and doctors' offices, they have significant drawbacks. A study prepared for the federal government highlighted the following drawbacks of group or scholarship trust RESPs:

- You must pay an enrolment fee and make contributions according to a pre-set schedule and stick to that schedule

22

(regardless of your change in financial circumstances) to remain enrolled in the plan.

• If you close a scholarship trust RESP before maturity for any reason, you forfeit the enrolment fee plus any investment gains and government Grant Money. So if you can't keep up with the pre-set contribution schedule, you lose. And no, you can't simply transfer funds to another plan. They won't let you.

• Some scholarship trust plans deny payments to students who are entitled to the benefits under government rules because that particular scholarship trust doesn't recognize all courses of study. If Darling chooses something outside the plan's parameters, she won't be able to use the money in the plan.

• If the scholarship trust plan is cancelled for any reason, you get your contributions back, net of fees and without the investment income. The Grant Money is also repaid to the government and cannot be earned back later if new contributions are made for the same beneficiary.

• Scholarship trusts have high fees. The report notes that in 2006, 20% of gross contributions went toward fees. Swoosh! There goes the free Grant Money!

The second question you're going to ask any provider you plan to work with is, **"Do you also automatically apply for all the grants to which my child may be entitled?"**

At my last count, there were over 65 companies selling RESPs in Canada. However, not all of these providers go beyond the basics in terms of making sure you get all the money you can from the government. I've already mentioned the Grant Money; all providers will automatically apply for that on your behalf. However, there are several other sources of extra money, including:

- an additional CESG above the basic 20%
- the Canada Learning Bond
- designated provincial programs currently available in Alberta and Quebec

Don't assume that your provider will gather up all this free money on your behalf. Ask if they will. And if they won't, find someone who will, unless you know for sure that you won't qualify for the extra money now or at any point in the future. Every free dollar you get is a dollar you don't have to take out of your cash flow, or a dollar your kid won't have to borrow and pay interest on down the road. Don't leave free money on the table!

The third question you're going to ask is, **"What fees do you charge?"** Most banks charge no fees for RESPs that invest in savings accounts, term deposits or GICs. For more sophisticated investments like mutual funds, individual stocks and bonds or indexed investments, expect to pay the typical fees associated with managing those investments. There's no hard or fast rule for what those fees should be; as long as your net return—the return earned after the fees are taken off—makes you happy, you're doing fine.

Find out if there is an application fee, a transfer fee or any other type of administrative fees before opening up the RESP. In my book, the best fee is no fee. But if you feel the service you're getting justifies the fee being charged, you're the customer and you get to make that call. Just GET IT IN WRITING. Don't assume that what you've been told will hold any water down the road. While fees may change over the life of your RESP, you don't want to start off with a provider who is going to juice you for every transaction you make. If the fees, or lack thereof, aren't clearly spelled out in your RESP contract, don't sign up.

GAIL'S TIP

A contract is a legal document, so make sure you read the fine print before you scribble your signature. If you don't understand something, ask for clarification. There is nothing to be embarrassed about in asking for more information. If you're shy, ask to take the paperwork home, where you can read through it slowly or ask a trusted friend or family member for help. Most financial contracts are full of gobbledygook and scare the pants off folks, which is why so many people sign without reading. That's a huge mistake.

Once you sign, you're going to have to live with whatever you agreed to, since a contract cannot be changed or broken unless both parties agree.

OPEN AN INDIVIDUAL RESP

No matter how many reasons your salesperson gives for opening a family plan, you should always open an individual RESP for your first child. Why? To avoid the RESP expiring with money still in it. EXPIRE?! An RESP can expire? You betcha.

All RESPs expire after 35 years. So if you have a mess of kids, or children with big age differences, a family plan could actually expire before the youngest child has the opportunity to use up the money. That means you would lose the Grant Money and the income earned inside the RESP.

But, Gail, 35 Years is a Really Long Time

Yes, it is. However, if you've accumulated a whack of money, the last thing you want is for that RESP to expire before your kids have finished getting their educations. Undergrad degrees often have to be supplemented with master's degrees or even PhDs, law school or med school, which can easily add up to 10 years of post-secondary education. Don't take any chances. Besides, you can always go from individual RESPs to a family plan, but you can't go the other way. Be on the safe side. Start with an individual RESP and move to a family plan if circumstances warrant the change.

Know When a Family Plan Works Best

While an individual RESP account can be set up by anyone (aunts, uncles, godparents, best friends), only a direct family member (parent, grandparent, great-grandparent or sibling) can set up and contribute to a family RESP. A family plan is almost identical to an individual plan except that more than one child can be the beneficiary of the plan.

So when would a family plan make sense? There are a couple of cases. The first is when one sibling decides not to pursue a post-secondary education. While that child's CESGs will have to be repaid to the government, the remaining money in the individual RESP—including all the income earned, even on the Grant Money you had to pay back—could be rolled into a family plan and used by other siblings who do choose to go on to further their educations.

The second case is when you started the RESP a little late and one child hasn't been able to grab all the Grant Money because he's "aged out"—he's over the age of 17 and Grant Money is no longer available. (More on this later.)

MAKE A CONTRIBUTION

You've done your research, gathered your documents and chosen your RESP provider. Now it's time to put some money away for Darling.

When you make a contribution to an RESP, you do NOT get a tax deduction for that contribution. However, as I mentioned earlier, all the income earned within the RESP grows tax-deferred and is only taxable as the bene-ficiary's income when it is withdrawn.

To get the maximum grant of $500 in any given year, you have to contribute $2,500 to an RESP in that year. A larger contribution won't get you more Grant Money unless you're catching up on unused CESG room. (We'll get into that next.)

The grant is calculated as 20% of your contribution up to the annual maximum of $500. **The maximum grant to which each child is entitled over the life of the RESP is $7,200.** So the maximum you must contribute to the RESP to get all the Grant Money to which Sonny or Darling is entitled is $36,000. If you squirrel away about $200 a month from when Darling is born until she's 15, you'll have grabbed all the Grant Money there is to grab.

If you can't swing the $200 a month it would take to get the maximum, that doesn't mean you shouldn't bother at all. Put in $100 a month, and your annual $1,200 will mean $240 in Grant Money. Can only manage $50 a month? Do it! You'll get $120 in Grant Money. That's money you get for free. Why would you pass up free money?

If aunts, uncles, grandparents or best friends want to open up their own RESP for your kid, they can do so as long as they've got Darling's or Sonny's SIN. They would be the plan owners, and Darling or Sonny would be the beneficiary. The maximum grant amount would still apply, so this should be a coordinated effort so you don't end up breaking the rules.

The maximum you can contribute to an RESP for any child is $50,000. If that limit is exceeded, the extra contributions will be taxed at the rate of 1% per month. It doesn't matter who's making the contributions or how many plans there are in that child's name—you can't exceed the $50,000 RESP lifetime limit per child. You can stick the money in all at once if you've got $50,000 and nothing much else to do with it. But if you do, you'll forgo almost all of the Grant Money, since the Grant Money is an annual award, and you can only capture up to two years' worth at any one time.

USE A CATCH-UP CESG

Not everyone has the foresight to start their kids' savings from the moment they land. You may not have known about RESPs. You may not have had any extra money while you were on maternity leave. If you have missed getting any of the Grant Money in earlier years because you made little or no contribution, the nice thing about the CESG is that you can catch up unused grant room later.

The maximum you can catch up in any one year is one additional year. So making a contribution higher than $5,000 would not earn you any more Grant Money.

The rules are a little complicated because once upon a

time, the maximum grant room was $2,000 a year (instead of the current $2,500), but that was changed in 2007. So if you're catching up for 2006 or earlier, when the old $2,000 limit was in place, that's the maximum you'll be able to contribute and have qualify for Grant Money for those years.

Okay, let's run through the rules and a couple of examples of how they work.

Catch-Up Rule #1

Did you miss contributions you could have made in 2007 and later? You can earn an extra 20%—up to $500 in a CESG—for contributions of up to $2,500 for one extra year.

Remember, the maximum you can catch up in any one year is one additional year. Don't be in such a hellfire rush to catch up that you end up missing out on the free Grant Money. Making a contribution higher than $5,000 would not earn you any more Grant Money.

Let's say Darling was born in 2007. She's seven years old now, and you haven't yet made a contribution for her. That means you have seven years for which you can catch up.

You can make your regular contribution of $2,500 for 2014, and the government will give you $500 in Grant Money. You can also make a catch-up contribution of up to $2,500 for one of those unused years prior to 2014 and you'll get an additional $500 in the CESG.

Catch-Up Rule #2

Did you miss contributions you could have made in 2006 or earlier? You can earn up to 20%—up to $400—in a CESG for contributions of up to $2,000 for catching up one year.

Let's say Sonny was born in 2004. He is now 10, and you haven't made any contributions for him yet. He has unused contributions for 2007 to 2013 that he could catch up at $2,500 a year for a CESG of $500 for each year. (You'd always catch up the years when you'd get the most money first, right? Duh!) He would also have three years of unused contributions before 2007—but he'd only be able to actually use two before he turned 18—which you could catch up at $2,000 a year for a grant of $400 for each year.

GET ALL THE MONEY YOU CAN

Along with the 20% CESG the government offers as an incentive for parents to save for their children's post-secondary education, there are additional grants available of 10% to 20% on the first $500 contributed based on family income. Regardless of who opens the RESP or makes the contribution, **the income of the primary caregiver** of the child will be assessed to determine if the child will get the additional grant.

Here's what you may be entitled to:

• If your family income is less than $43,562, then you can grab an additional 20% grant (up to $100) on the first $500 of your contribution.
• If your family income is between $43,562 and $87,123, then you'll be entitled to an additional 10% (instead of the 20% mentioned in the previous point), or $50, on the first $500 of your contribution.

Let's say your family makes under $43,562, and with help from your friends and relatives, you put just $600 in an RESP for Sonny. You'd receive:

• $120 (or 20%) in Grant Money, plus
• $100 in additional Grant Money on the first $500 you contributed

So you could put in $600 and you'd receive $220 in Grant Money, for a total of $820 going to work for your child's future education. Now answer me this: Where else can you get a 37% return on your money just for setting aside $50 a month?

It will be up to you to make sure that your RESP provider applies for both parts of the CESG on your behalf.

GAIL'S TIP

The family income required to claim the extra Grant Money changes every year, so you must check to see the current year's family income limits. You can do so at www.canlearn.ca. I'm writing this in 2013, so I'm using 2013 numbers. To find out your net family income, check:

- your Notice of Assessment (if you're married or have a common-law partner, you must add the two net incomes on Line 236)
- your Canada Child Tax Benefit Notice of Determination
- your Goods and Services Tax Credit Notice of Determination

Alternatively, you can check "My Account," available at the Canada Revenue Agency website.

Provincial Plans

If you lived in Alberta or Quebec when your child was born, provincial grants may also be available to you.

Alberta

(At the time of writing, the ACESPG was "under review to determine the future of the program." I've included what was in place just in case it is kept as is. But you should google "Alberta Centennial" to get the most recent information available from their website.)

The Alberta Centennial Education Savings Plan Grant (ACESPG) offers an additional $500 in Grant Money to add to your RESP—on top of the federal Grant Money—for every child born to Alberta residents in 2005 and after.

Additional grants of $100 are available to children in the years in which they turn 8, 11 and 14 (after January 1, 2005), provided those kids are attending school in Alberta or attending a school that meets the Ministry of Enterprise and Advanced Education's criteria. Home-schooled children are also eligible.

A minimum of $100 must have been invested in an RESP within one year prior to any application for an ACESPG. And parents or guardians must be residents of Alberta at the time of application. To get the $500 grant, the application must be submitted before your child turns six. To get each of the subsequent three grants, separate applications must be submitted within six years following the child's 8th, 11th and 14th birthdays. If the beneficiary does not go on to post-secondary schooling, the ACESPG must be returned to the Government of Alberta. Residents of Alberta can call 1-866-515-ACES (2237) to learn more about the ACESPG.

That means as long as you make at least a $100 contribution to an RESP one year before your child's 6th, 8th, 11th and 14th birthdays, you can claim a total of $800 in Grant Money from the ACESPG. So if you live in Alberta, and Sonny is turning 8 (or 6 or 11 or 14) this year, ask your plan provider for the application you'll need to claim this Grant Money. Once approved, your funds will be automatically deposited.

Quebec

In Quebec, the Québec Education Savings Incentive (QESI) pays a refundable tax credit directly to an RESP for beneficiaries under 18 who are residents of Quebec on December 31 of the tax year. So if you live in Quebec on the last day of the year, regardless of how long you've lived there, you can apply for the refundable tax credit for kids under 18.

The amount paid is equal to 10% of the net contributions paid into the RESP over a year, to a maximum of $250. So if you put $2,000 into an RESP in 2013, Revenu Québec will pay $200 into the RESP in 2014.

In essence, if you live in Quebec, your Grant Money ends up adding 30% to your contribution instead of the standard 20% CESG. So if you made a contribution of $2,500, you'd get $500 through the federal CESG and an additional $250 from the QESI for a total of $750 in Grant Money. Geez, that's a sweet deal.

As of 2008, you are allowed to carry forward a $250 grant, so you can actually claim up to $500 in QESI grants if you contribute $5,000 and there are years since 2008 for which you haven't made a claim. As with the CESG, you can only catch up one year at a time.

To help low-income families, the QESI also offers:

• a 10% bonus award on the first $500 in contributions each year for families with a net income of $42,707 or less
• a 5% bonus award on the first $500 each year for families with a net income between $42,708 and $85,414

The total QESI is capped at a lifetime limit of $3,600. For information, call Services Québec at 1-877-644-4545.

No Money to Save?

Here's something I hear all the time: "Gail, I don't have an extra penny to spare for an RESP. I just don't make enough money."

Hey, what if I told you Sonny could get up to $2,000 in free money from the government? Would you be interested?

If Sonny was born on January 1, 2004, or after, and your family receives the National Child Benefit supplement, Sonny is entitled to the Canada Learning Bond. All you have to do is open up an RESP for him and the feds will deposit $500 in the first year and up to an additional $1,500 more by the time Sonny turns 15. Here are the details:

• you don't have to put any of your own money into an RESP to get the Canada Learning Bond
• you'd receive $500 immediately
• you'd receive $100 each year up until Sonny's 15
• they'll even spot you an extra $25 to help cover the cost of opening up the RESP

This $2,000 and all the income earned on it must be used for post-secondary education. It can be university. It can be college. It can be a trade school or an apprentice-ship program. It can be full- or part-time. If your child does not continue education after high school, the feds will grab their money back.

Now you no longer have the excuse of "no money." Go and open up an RESP today! Just make sure that your RESP provider is one that is willing to apply for the Canada Learning Bond on your behalf.

WHAT HAPPENS IF I WITHDRAW CONTRIBUTIONS I'VE MADE?

When you withdraw money from your child's RESP (out-side of the approved withdrawal process when your child goes to school), the RESP provider is required to repay any Grant Money received on those contributions.

All RESP contributions are broken down into two pools: "assisted contributions," which qualified for the Grant Money, and "unassisted contributions," for which the RESP received no Grant Money.

Early withdrawals of contributions are always paid from the assisted pool first. The amount repayable is equal to 20% of the withdrawal, up to the total accumulated CESGs. So that would be $500 for every $2,500 contrib-uted, or $400 for every $2,000 contributed or caught up for years prior to 2007.

GAIL'S TIP

....

Remember, only the first $36,000 in RESP contributions qualifies for the Grant Money. The remaining $14,000 that you're entitled to contribute—since the lifetime maximum contribution is $50,000—won't earn a grant but will grow on a tax-deferred basis. If you have the money to contribute, doing so will ensure a bigger pool of funds will be available when your kid heads off to the halls of higher learning. And with costs projected to rise dramatically, every penny you can sock away to earn another penny will be much appreciated later on.

....

HOW OTHERS CAN
HELP BUILD SAVINGS

....

If you have family and friends who wish to contribute directly to an RESP for Darling and Sonny, make sure everyone knows that the government tallies contributions for a child in order to enforce the limits and maximum amounts. So it doesn't matter who opens the RESP or how many plans are in Darling's name (using her SIN)—the following rules can't be broken:

• If the annual grant-eligible contribution amount ($2,500 per year) is exceeded, the excess contributions aren't eligible for grants.

• The lifetime contribution limit is $50,000, and if that limit is exceeded, the extra contributions will be taxed at the rate of 1% per month.

You will know if a plan has been set up for your child by someone else because RESP providers must notify minor beneficiaries' parents within 90 days, providing the name of the subscriber. So if your sister sets up an RESP for Darling as a gift, you'll know just how much she's put in, so there's no risk that the RESP contribution limits will be exceeded.

Remember, the money in an RESP belongs to the person who put it in—the subscriber—right up until it's taken out for use by the beneficiary. When a contribution to an RESP is withdrawn, any Grant Money earned on that contribution must be returned to the government. And that grant room is gone for good.

Let's say your mother made a contribution for Sonny of $1,200 each year for three years, on which he earned $240 a year in grant room. Having run into financial trouble, your mom cashes out the $3,600 RESP, returning the $720 in Grant Money claimed. That grant room is gone. You can't make a replacement contribution and try and claim that grant room back, because the system won't let you. Sucks, eh?

Remember, the same rules apply if a subscriber dies: since he owns the RESP, the RESP account is part of his estate. Unless an alternate subscriber has been named, the RESP may have to be collapsed and the net money divided up as part of the estate settlement. Tell relatives that if their RESP provider seems unwilling to allow them to name an alternate subscriber, they can do so in their wills.

Perhaps because I'm a control freak, if family and friends wanted to help me, I'd ask for the money directly and make the contributions myself (as the subscriber) to ensure the money would still be there in 18 years when it was finally time to use it. I'd be some ticked if my baby girl or boyo lost out on CESGs because Auntie or Uncle decided to take their money back, those grants had to be repaid and that grant room was lost forever.

GROW THE RESP CONTRIBUTIONS

Like an RRSP or a Tax-Free Savings Account (TFSA), an RESP is simply a "plan" with a number that tells the taxman to keep his sticky paws off the return being earned. An RESP is NOT an investment. For the money you put into the plan to make more money, you will have to choose an investment.

There's the tried-and-true and completely safe savings account that will earn you a small return but carries no risk. Or you can use a GIC once you have enough money—typically $1,000 to $5,000, depending on the financial institution. You'll earn a little more in interest for locking up your money for a specific term. If you're more knowledgeable and experienced, you might go with a mutual fund, direct investing in an index or stocks that produce dividends.

Anything you can hold in your TFSA or RRSP can be held in your RESP. The thing to keep front and centre is that as your child gets closer to using the money, you need to move from growth-oriented investments (if you have them) to less volatile investments, so the money is there and available when you need it.

As soon as Sonny and Darling hit middle school, you should be looking at moving to fixed-income investments. If the markets are off slightly, don't sweat it; you still have some time to wait out a recovery. But if the markets are doing well, don't get lulled into a sense that markets will always go up. Take your profits and move to investment options that will guarantee your money is around when Sonny and Darling need to start forking over tuition.

OTHER WAYS TO SAVE

While an RESP is the single best way to save for school, that's only true as long as you're getting the maximum Grant Money. To earn the max, you'll have to set aside $2,500 a year. If you're catching up, you can put in up to $5,000 a year in an RESP (the current year's contribution and up to one other year's contribution) and get $1,000 in Grant Money. If you want to save beyond that $2,500 or $5,000 a year, the RESP isn't necessarily the best deal going.

Consider Your TFSA

If you have room to save for Sonny and Darling using a TFSA, use it. You can't open one up for a child, because you have to be a Canadian resident and 18 or older to have one. But you could allocate a part of your TFSA room to saving for school.

You can save up to $5,500 a year in a TFSA (in 2013, the limit was up $500 from previous years). Limits are going to be indexed to inflation in $500 increments, so watch for more increases in limits over time.

You can have as many TFSAs as you wish, so you could open one up just to hold your school savings, but the $5,500 contribution limit applies across all accounts.

As with RESPs, contributions to a TFSA are NOT tax deductible. But while an RESP's income is tax-deferred—Sonny and Darling will have to pay tax on the income when they pull it out—all the income earned inside a TFSA is earned tax-free, making it a better choice than bumping up your RESP contribution, providing you have the room.

Since contribution room can be carried forward, if there are years for which you haven't made TFSA contributions, you can catch up. Let's say you only saved $2,000 in 2013; in 2014, your limit will be $9,000 ($5,500 for 2014 and $3,500 carried forward from 2013). Got a good bonus this year and want to boost the kids' school savings? Use the extra room in your TFSA to sock it away.

Any investment you can buy for your RESP can be

held inside a TFSA, including stocks, bonds, a GIC and mutual funds, so your investment options aren't limited. And since you can make a beneficiary designation (everywhere in Canada except Quebec) on your TFSA to avoid probate costs, you can name your child directly, making it even better than an RESP for estate-planning purposes.

In-Trust Accounts

Setting up a formal trust can be expensive and, for the purpose of saving for school, not very financially efficient. The alternative is a less formal "in-trust account," through which you set aside money for a minor child. If you are going to buy capital gains–based investments, an in-trust account may be a good option. Instead of just opening an account in your kid's name, this account—be it a savings account or an investment account—would say "Mommy Dearest in trust for Darling Daughter." Then all capital gains are taxed in Darling's hands at a lower rate.

Once upon a time, in-trust accounts were a better alternative to RESPs—I set up in-trust accounts for Alex and Malcolm before RESPs became the good deal they are now—but the taxman got tired of watching people put the money in and take the money out, and put the money in and take the money out, and put the money in . . . well, you get my drift. So they decided to come down hard on "in-trust accounts" that were not functioning as they should.

To pass code, the person who puts the money in cannot be the person holding the money in trust for Sonny and Darling. So if Mommy wants to be the trustee (as in Donna Dee in trust for Darling Dee), then all the money must come from Daddy's resources (and not joint resources). This is to ensure that the person giving up the money—putting it in trust for Darling—doesn't have any control over the money from that point forward.

Technically, kids can act as both the contributor and beneficiary of a trust, but the trustee cannot be a minor. The taxman doesn't much care who the trustee part of the equation is, but the feds are pretty strict on who puts the money in, and on ensuring that once in, the money remains the child's assets.

One of the downsides of an in-trust account is that tax on all interest or dividend income earned in the account must be paid by the person who originally gifted the money. Only capital gains are taxed in the hands of the beneficiary (the child). So if you're going to set up one of these puppies for Darling or Sonny, it should be early in their lives when they have a long-term investment horizon (more than 10 years until they'll need the money) and can take advantage of equity investing. If you don't have the time or stomach for stock market investing, skip the in-trust account, since you'll derive no tax benefit.

There are loads of ways to save for school for your children. And some of those ways will get you free money. All you have to do is decide that putting a little sumthin'

sumthin' aside for your children's future is a priority. Yes, you may have to go without coffee twice a week, negotiate a better deal with your cable company or forgo your shopping indulgence to have the money to set aside for Sonny or Darling. Hey, that's what being a parent is all about: making choices that give your kids the best start in life that you can swing. It may not always feel great to go without so you can come up with $25, $50 or $100 a month to save for school. Ask yourself this question: "Are my personal indulgences more important than my responsibility to my child?" If the answer is no, it's time to get saving!

TWO

Taking Money Out

· ·

You've been saving for years, and now Darling Daughter and Sonny Boy are headed off to school. It's time to take the money out of the RESP.

Before we look at how to take money out of an RESP, let's review how the money went in.

When you put money from your pocket into an RESP, you made a contribution—that's called the "contribution amount." Bear with me as I get really finicky here; I'm not trying to insult your intelligence, but the rules have been made overly complicated and confusing by the language the government uses.

Okay, so the money you put into the plan is the "contribution amount." Any money in the plan that didn't come from your pocket is the "non-contribution amount." That would be the interest, dividends or capital gains you may have earned on the investments you chose for the RESP, and the CESG (or Grant Money) your children received from the government to boost their savings. Ditto money you received as a Canada Learning Bond or through a provincial program.

HOW MONEY COMES OUT FOR SCHOOL

When it comes time to take money OUT of the RESP, it comes out in one of two ways:

• The contribution amount comes out as a Post-Secondary Education Payment (PSE). There are no restrictions on how much you can take, and there are no taxes that must be paid on this money, since you didn't get a tax deduction when you put the money in. The only rule to ensure you don't affect the Grant Money is that your child must be enrolled in school when the PSE is withdrawn.
• The non-contribution amount comes out as an Educational Assistance Payment (EAP), and you may only take up to $5,000 in the first 13 weeks of full-time enrolment in school; after that 13 weeks, there's no limit. These withdrawals are taxable in your child's hands.

For most students, it makes sense to first take the majority of the RESP money out as an EAP, pulling on the non-contribution amount in the early years, for two reasons:

- When a student's income from other sources is lowest, they'll pay less in taxes on the EAP.
- The non-contribution amount is the part of the RESP that's made up of Grant Money and income—be it interest on a GIC, or dividends or capital gains on a mutual fund—and is the portion of an RESP that has taxes and fees attached if a student doesn't use it all. So it makes sense to use up this portion of the RESP as quickly as possible. If you wait, and Sonny doesn't complete school, leaving income and Grant Money in the plan, that money may be heavily taxed and penalized. Using it up early in Sonny's student life means that only the contribution amount remains in the plan. And that contribution amount can be withdrawn at any time with no taxes or penalties. (There will be more shortly on what happens if an RESP isn't used.)

Check with your RESP provider to see if they automatically default withdrawals to 100% EAP. Many do, and this is the preferable option. If they don't, you'll have to direct them to make the early payouts EAPs.

GAIL'S TIP

....

While you'll never receive a statement showing the breakdown of how much you've put in versus how much Grant Money or earnings there are in the RESP (wouldn't THAT be a good idea?), your plan manager has the details, and you should ask him or her to make sure you're on the right side of the rules each year. The plan manager's only responsibility is to accurately report the amounts taken on the appropriate tax documents. Remember, in the eyes of the taxman, it doesn't matter who buggers stuff up, YOU are always on the hook! So ask your plan manager for the details and make a note of them on your file, comparing them to the tax slips received at the end of each year.

HOW TO TAKE MONEY FROM AN RESP

You won't be able to get your hands on money in an RESP until Sonny and Darling receive their letters of acceptance from school. Most RESP providers have specific requirements for proof of enrolment, so make sure you know what you have to give them to get to the money. When Alex was going off to school, I just had to pony up her online registration and the subsequent registration confirmation that she received, along with her offer of admission. But sometimes you have to get a special form filled out by the university, so ask.

You can direct that the money from the RESP be sent to you as the subscriber, to the student (the beneficiary) or directly to the institution. If you're planning on paying for living expenses beyond residence and tuition from the RESP, and you're not convinced your kid is savvy enough to handle a whack of cash all at once, you can have the money sent to you and then dole it out monthly. Since the money is technically still yours, the student can't ask the RESP provider for payments from an RESP. Only you, as subscriber, can do this.

Remember that the government has put a little hitch into the system to try and stop scoundrels from grabbing Grant Money and then absconding without going to school. The hitch is that you can only take $5,000 from the RESP as an EAP in the first 13 weeks of school (so $5,000 from non-contribution money). After that, as long as your annual EAP requests are under $20,000 a year, you don't have to provide any documentation to show your expenses for school are "reasonable." If you must take more than the $20,000, you'll either have to document those expenses or take the money as a PSE to avoid having to document every penny you're spending. And if you'll need more than that $5,000 in the first 13 weeks of school, take it as a PSE.

GAIL'S TIP

When Alex first went to university, I was confused about the distinction between the PSE and the EAP. Her tuition exceeded the $5,000 we were allowed to withdraw under the EAP, and my understanding was that her withdrawals had to be limited to that $5,000 for her first 13 weeks of school. So we paid only the $5,000 and had to pay interest on the tuition that remained unpaid. Ugh! My plan manager led me to believe that was the only way. Wrong! What I could have done was taken the $5,000 as an EAP and then taken the rest as a PSE, using the contribution money. You live and learn! It was this experience with Alex's RESP that got me up on the rules and became the impetus for writing this book. It's important that you understand how the money is "viewed" by the taxman, so you can use the plan to full advantage. You can't rely on your RESP plan manager to explain these rules to you.

KNOW HOW YOU CAN USE RESP MONEY

RESPs can be used for a wide range of educational costs—from colleges and universities, to trade schools and apprenticeships—and the school doesn't have to be in Canada. Schools around the world qualify. The Master List of Designated Educational Institutions is updated regularly and contains all the educational institutions where students are eligible to use their RESP money. (Go to www.canlearn.ca/eng/tools/designated/index.shtml for a complete list by province.)

Tuition isn't the only thing you can use the RESP dollars for. You can use the money to buy books. You can use the money to buy a laptop. In fact, as long as Sonny and Darling are enrolled in school, they can draw on their

RESPs for just about anything they need, from rent or residence costs to food or transportation, as long as it's within the RESP provider's parameters. You'll have to check with your RESP provider directly to find out what's on their "approved" list. If you don't like the limits your RESP provider may be putting on how the money can be used, you're free to shop around, find a provider with rules that suit you and transfer your RESP. However, RESP transfers are not permitted once a withdrawal has been made from the RESP.

KNOW HOW INCOME TAXES WORK WITH AN RESP

Even if Sonny has a very limited income while at school, it makes sense to manage how he takes money from his RESPs so that he pays the least amount of tax possible. Remember, when money is withdrawn as a PSE, that money isn't taxable because it comes from the principal portion of the RESP. However, when EAPs are taken, they are part of Sonny's taxable income for that year and a T4A slip will be issued in his name for any EAPs made during that year. You want to be careful how much money you take out as EAPs if your child is also working, in case the EAPs, which are taxable, will push him into a higher tax bracket.

Here are the basics: Every Canadian has a personal exemption amount, which is the amount they can earn before they have to start paying tax. For 2013, the first $11,038 in income wasn't taxable federally, so Darling and Sonny could have had that much income from all sources—work, EAP withdrawals or any other forms of income—before having to pay a penny in tax. Google "personal exemption amount Canada," including the year you're in, to find the most current amount.

GAIL'S TIP

Did Darling get a scholarship or bursary while at school? Don't let the T4A slip she got fool you into thinking that money is taxable. It's not. While students will receive a T4A tax information slip for scholarships or bursaries they've received, if it relates to enrolment in a program that entitles them to the education tax credit (I'll cover this shortly), the amount does not need to be reported on their income tax return. It is, in effect, fully tax-exempt.

Added to the personal exemption amount are the tuition and education tax credits that can further reduce any taxes payable. Each year that Sonny and Darling are in school, they'll receive a tax certificate from their university or college that shows the fees paid that are eligible for the tuition tax credit. Any exam fees paid as a requirement for obtaining professional status, or for licensing or certification as a tradesperson, may also be eligible for the tuition tax credit. Check with the educational institution, professional association or provincial ministry when you're signing up for the exam.

That amount can be claimed on the tax return as a non-refundable credit, which means it can be used to reduce taxes owed but won't generate a refund. The tax credit is calculated at the lowest federal tax rate percentage. Currently, that's 15%. If Sonny's tuition for his first year is $10,000, he will be able to reduce his income tax by $1,500 using the non-refundable tax credit for tuition ($10,000 × 15% = $1,500).

Students are also eligible for an education tax credit for the amount of time they spend in school each year. The rule is you can claim $400 a month for each whole or part month in a year that you're enrolled full-time. Part-time students can claim $120 per month. Unlike the tuition credit, the education tax credit *is* refundable, so if Darling is in school full-time for eight months of the year—from September to April—she can claim $400 × 8 = $3,200, which will result in a $480 refund ($3,200 × 15%).

Students can also claim a textbook tax credit of $65 for each month they are enrolled in a course that entitles them to a full-time education tax credit. This tax credit, like the tuition tax credit, is non-refundable.

If Sonny can't use his non-refundable tax credits because his income is too low, he can carry them forward or transfer them to a partner, parent or grandparent.

GAIL'S TIP

To qualify as full-time in Canada, the course of study has to be at least three successive weeks with a minimum of 10 hours of instruction per week. For foreign schools, the program has to last at least 13 weeks. Part-time enrolment is also allowed in Canada. Eligible programs must have at least 12 hours of course work each month and must run for a minimum of three consecutive weeks.

DON'T MISALLOCATE CESGS

If you have a family plan set up, make sure that you don't end up withdrawing more than the maximum of $7,200 in Grant Money allowed for each beneficiary. If you attempt to go over the limit, the grants will be returned to the government. Your RESP plan manager should be keeping track of how much Grant Money is paid out to each beneficiary, so ask for an update and make your withdrawals based on that information.

The taxman doesn't care who "earned" the Grant Money, just that you don't go over the $7,200 lifetime limit per child. Why does this matter? Let's say you have a family plan for Sonny and Darling. Sonny has gone off to university, but you hadn't contributed enough to his RESP to reach the lifetime grant limit, so he only has $6,700 in Grant Money in the RESP. He isn't eligible to receive any more Grant Money because he is over 17, so you can't make any further contributions to the family RESP on his behalf. You *can*, however, make a contribution of $2,500 for Darling, which would add $500 in Grant Money to your family plan. You could then withdraw up to the $7,200 limit of Grant Money for Sonny to use ($6,700 from his Grant Money and $500 from Darling's). Why would you want to do this? If Darling decides not to go to school, you can withdraw her portion of the RESP, which would come from the principal, and she could use that to jump-start a business, make a down payment on a home, or to do anything else that she wants with the money. In the meantime, Sonny got all the Grant Money he could use. If she *does* want to go to school, you can just use more of the contribution funds to pay for her expenses.

IF AN RESP ISN'T USED

If you've been saving for years and Darling decides not to use the money for school, not only will you be disappointed, you're also going to have to do some fancy footwork to avoid paying taxes and fees.

If Sonny can use the money in the RESP for school, you can transfer the RESP to him. Or you can transfer the money to any other child, as long as that child is connected to you, as the subscriber, by blood or adoption (so stepchildren don't count). The replacement beneficiary will be able to keep and use the CESGs paid into a family plan as long as he or she is under the age of 21 and doesn't exceed the lifetime limit of $7,200.

What if there's no one to whom you can transfer the unused RESP? Here's what happens next:

• You can withdraw any contributions you made without any consequences. Since those contributions were made in after-tax dollars—you did not get a deduction for them—you can take them back at any time.
• The CESGs, Canada Learning Bond and provincial benefits (in the case of Alberta and Quebec) paid into the RESP on behalf of the child will be returned to the government automatically by your plan provider.

The remaining money in the plan is made up of the return you earned on the investments inside the RESP. Remember, this money has been allowed to grow tax-deferred—without you having to pay any taxes on each year's earnings—for the benefit of your kids' education. If that's not what the money is going to be used for, the government will want its pound of flesh.

First, the good news: up to $50,000 of this growth money can be transferred to the subscriber's RRSP or to the subscriber's spouse's RRSP without penalty as long as there is sufficient contribution room.

GAIL'S TIP

....

Withdrawals from an RESP can be made up to six months after a child stops attending school. As long as the money is being used for approved "school-related" expenses, you can pull money out under the same rules used for the original EAPs.

Let's say Sonny graduates and there is still $3,000 in income (and by income, I mean the Grant Money and whatever interest, dividends or capital gains your investments earned, not the original contributions) remaining in the RESP. Sonny's grandparents helped him by paying his rent while he was living off campus, to the tune of $500 a month for two years. Sonny can make a final withdrawal from the RESP of that $3,000, claiming it as repayment of the rent his grandparents paid on his behalf.

While you might not think your children will graduate from school with a whole hell of a lot of money left in their RESPs, consider the kids who decide to leave school before they've used all the money. Having the option of taking some or most of the income earned inside the plan as a final payment during the six months after they have left school would mean not having to run into the penalties and taxes applied later on.

....

For individual and family RESPs, you'll have to wait until the plan has been open for 10 years and the beneficiaries are all over the age of 21 before you can execute the rollover to your RRSP. For group RESPs, you won't get this option unless you are first able to transfer the group RESP to an individual RESP.

GAIL'S TIP

....

Since an RESP can remain in place for up to 35 years, if you do not currently have enough RRSP contribution room, hold off on making RRSP contributions for a few years, so that you build up some room to make the transfer possible.

....

Now, the bad news: if neither you nor your spouse has enough RRSP room to accommodate the $50,000 rollover, or if there is more than $50,000 in accumulated earnings in the RESP, any remaining money will be fully taxable at the subscriber's marginal tax rate. Plus, there is an additional penalty of 20% on the withdrawn amount. So if you're in the 25% tax bracket, you would end up paying 25% + 20% = 45% in taxes on the money withdrawn. Ouch!

If you don't want to get bitten with those taxes and penalties, you need to keep a firm eye on what's going on with your RESP. Make sure the Grant Money and the income earned within the plan is paid out first. That'll leave only the original contributions, which can be withdrawn without taxes or penalties. If your kid looks ready to bolt from school, and you have other children who might benefit, move the individual plan to a family plan.

Taking money out of an RESP in the most tax-efficient way takes some planning. And making sure all the Grant Money and income is used up first should be a priority, so that if there is money left over (you never know!) it won't be penalized coming out of the RESP. If you're feeling a little overwhelmed, find a friend, co-worker, accountant or financial adviser who gets what's going on and ask for some help in making the plan. There's no shame in asking for guidance if you're feeling muddled. Put your pride away and ask for some help so you make the best decisions you can for your children.

THREE

Making the Money Last

. . . .

Our kids grow up and head off to school, and there's so much we didn't teach them. Can they cook a meal for themselves? Do they know how to stretch a dollar at the supermarket? Can they sew on a button, hem a skirt, fix a zipper?

Preparing our children for their first big adventure without us means we have to get into some serious conversations. How much money will they borrow to see them through school? Will they get one of those credit cards that banks throw at young adults before they've even started to earn a living? Do they even know the difference between a need and a want, or have they gotten so used to "our" lifestyle that they think they're entitled to maintain the same standard of living as they go through school?

BORROWING FOR SCHOOL
....

In the best of all worlds, there'd be enough money in your kids' RESPs to see them all the way through school. Ah, yes, the best of worlds. Sadly, we sometimes fall a little short of perfect, in which case, kids may have to borrow some money.

If you let your kids go into the student loan system blindly, you're setting them up to come out of school buried in debt and incapable of putting a roof over their own heads. Think of a conversation as the first step in ensuring that Sonny and Darling are capable of living independently. If you don't have this conversation, you shouldn't be surprised when your Mini-Me moves home and never wants to leave!

Deciding how much to borrow is a business decision. Treat it as such. Don't bother with all the yada yada about deserving an education or expanding minds or all the other bullcrap people use as an excuse for digging a debt hole. Take the emotion out of the exercise and do the numbers based on cold, hard facts.

Don't let anyone tell you that a university or college education guarantees big money. Every career choice has its own income scale, and knowing the potential earning capacity makes sense so you don't end up overpaying for it. Teachers can make more or less than lawyers, dentists, call-centre workers, engineers, writers and nurses. Before kids dive into more debt than they'll be able to afford to repay, they must figure out how much income they're going to earn in the early stages of a career . . . so in years 1 to 10.

How much money will Darling and Sonny likely make when they graduate? The Ontario Ministry of Training, Colleges and Universities (www.tcu.gov.on.ca/eng/) has a breakdown of graduation rates and employment rates by course. Have a look through it to get more familiar with what's in demand. Alberta Learning Information Service (http://alis.alberta.ca/index.html) offers a FABULOUS resource that tells you what a job entails, what education you need and what you'll likely earn (in Alberta). Look under "Wages & Salaries."

If this were a business loan, lenders would want to know what kind of income the business would produce to see if it could afford the loan repayments. Help Sonny and Darling go into this student loan decision with the same perspective. Here's what I told Alex: "YOU are your business, and your income, once it starts, will play a big role in how long it'll take to get out of debt and in the interest you'll pay while you do."

The Gail Rule for borrowing for school is this: Darling and Sonny should borrow no more than one year's net salary; otherwise, the debt repayment schedule becomes so heavy that it's impossible to get out of debt without paying a ton in interest.

Here's what happens after school, so you have a good sense of why it's so important to follow the Gail Rule of no more than one year's net salary in student loans: Let's say Darling decides to be a pharmacist when she's all grown up. She'll net about $52,000 a year, or $4,333 a month. Assuming that she follows my rule and that her interest rate is 7.25% and she chooses the 10-year repayment schedule, her monthly payment would be $631, which represents about 15% of her net income. But taking 10 years to repay the student loan means Darling will also pay $23,708 in interest. So her education will actually cost $75,708, or 46% more than when she left school.

Sonny, on the other hand, decides to pay that loan off in five years. Yay, Sonny. He will pay $11,262 in interest, less than half of what Darling had to pay. But because his repayment time frame is shorter, his payments will be higher: $1,054, which means he'll be spending 24% of his income (almost a quarter of it) on student loan repayments.

The less debt your kids leave school with, the better their lives will be. If they hope to have a car, buy a home, have a family, go on a vacation or do anything else that involves having a life during those years of student loan repayment, less debt is better.

Figuring out how much you'll have to repay is simply a matter of knowing your interest rate and how long you want to take to pay off the loan. Here are the rough mechanics: Sonny has a $28,000 loan at 6% and wants to have the student loan paid off in 36 months. First, calculate the interest: $28,000 × 6% ÷ 12 (months) = $140. That's the interest part of your monthly payment.

Now, calculate the principal repayment: Take your total principal of $28,000 and divide it by the number of months you want to take to pay off the loan, in this case 36. So, $28,000 ÷ 36 = $777.78. We'll call it $778.

Add the principal amount of $778 to $140 in interest, and your monthly payment is $918. That's a good indicator of what your monthly payment will be on the loan. It'll actually be a little less, since interest is calculated on a declining balance (as you pay off your loan, the principal goes down, so the amount of interest goes down). The Government of Canada website, www.canlearn.ca, offers a loan repayment calculator to take the math out of the exercise, if you're number-challenged.

Please, please, before your kids head off and borrow too much money, make them look at their student loan debt in relation to their earning ability. That's common sense, right? But few people understand this relationship, which is why so many are buried in debt and unable to get on with their lives.

FINDING MONEY WHEREVER YOU CAN

In the years leading up to university or college, if you find you were not able to save as much as you would have liked in the RESP, you're going to have to get creative. And you should encourage Darling and Sonny to do the same. One of the best ways to help fund school is to use the thousands of scholarships offered to Canadian students. It's a sad reality that gobs of this free money go unused either because students don't know about it or because their grades aren't high enough to qualify.

If your kids have crappy grades coming out of high school, university and college may not be for them, plain and simple. Trying to force-fit them into an academic life isn't in anyone's best interest.

As for not knowing about the scholarships available, there's an easy remedy. Go to http://scholarshipscanada .com, www.studentawards.com or www.aucc.ca and check out what's available. Sometimes people tell me that it's too much "trouble" applying for the smaller scholarships. Really, you're prepared to let your young adults walk away from free money just because they don't want to write the essay or fill out the application? Then don't complain about what school is costing!

IS A CREDIT CARD A GOOD IDEA?

One of the questions I get most often from parents is this: "Should my child apply for a credit card while at university or college?" Y'know, it depends on your child.

There's no easier time to get a credit card than when you're in college or university. Ironically, even though Darling doesn't have a job, credit card companies will be rushing to sign her up because she's a good long-term prospect, what with that expensive education she's getting and all. And, yes, assuming she's not a money moron, she should take advantage of the opportunity. If she waits until after graduation, she may find it much harder to qualify. (Again, ironic, isn't it?)

Darling can use her credit card to cover essential expenses like food, as long as she pays the bill in full every month. That will help her establish her credit identity. The proviso is that she also learns the importance of tracking her expenses.

The right to use a credit card comes with the responsibility of keeping track of every penny spent and paying the balance in full every month. Offer her a notebook to use as a spending journal and show her how to keep a running balance that reflects the reality of her spending and her bank account. When she gets money, she adds it to her balance. When she spends money—in cash, using a debit card, using her shiny new credit card or by writing cheques—she deducts it from her balance. The point is to always know what's left in the bank, and the spending journal will go a long way in helping with impulse control.

If Darling is impulsive and shows no ability to manage the details of a credit card, then it may be more of a trap than a tool. If she just needs some practice, a card with a really low limit—say $250—means she won't be able to dig too deep a hole. Remind her that she can do as much damage as good with a credit card. If she doesn't make her payments on time, it'll be recorded on her credit history for longer than she is in school.

LIVING THROUGH SCHOOL

Being a student means having limited resources, so you better send your young 'uns off with realistic expectations. They'll eat cheap food. They'll have to wear their clothes until they are threadbare. They'll live in tight quarters. Hey, that's the life of the poor student. And maybe it'll help them focus on what they don't want for the rest of their lives.

If your kids are going to school to par-taay, to drink their faces off, or take six years to get a three-year degree, why would you want to support that?

School is serious business. And it's expensive. When my daughter did her undergrad at McMaster, it was an $18,000-a-year expense. And lest you think that's because she's a princess, think again. Remember, she shared a house (a regular-sized house) with six other people. Yup, every single room (except bathrooms and kitchens) had been turned into a bedroom. Those kids were living lean.

Living the poor student life is not forever. Short-term pain for long-term gain, that's school. If kids do it right, they'll graduate knowing what they need to make a life for themselves. They'll have learned to be frugal. They'll have learned to prioritize. And they'll be strong because they had some rough spots but got through them.

That's not to say that there aren't lots of people who graduate from school without good sense. I've met them. People still living off their parents. People who prioritize the car they drive over the food they put on the table.

People who, after years of college, trade school or university, succeeded in NOT GROWING UP. Poor things. Poor things, the people who have to live with them.

But that's not what you want for your children, right? You've decided to help Sonny and Darling do this whole post-secondary thing right. You've talked to them about making plans for a career. You've encouraged them to apply for scholarships. You've been saving for tuition. Now it's time to teach your soon-to-be-independent young adults how to manage their money. **And, Mom and Dad, DO NOT withdraw money from your retirement savings plan to fund your children's education.**

Managing the Money while at School

Money comes to kids in two ways: in a lump sum and in a steady flow. Expenses work the same way when you're a student.

If Sonny and Darling worked all summer and over the years leading up to their next schooling adventure, they'd have a lump sum. Ditto scholarship money, bursaries and gifts from family. And then there's the RESP money.

If you don't want your kids blowing through their money faster than grass goes through a goose, they have to make a plan. On my website, www.gailvazoxlade.com, under "Resources," I have an Excel spreadsheet called "Student Lump-Sum Money Worksheet," which you can download; or you can make your own (see page 72 for a sample).

Student Lump-Sum Money Worksheet

LUMP-SUM INCOME	
Savings from Summer Job	$
Scholarships	$
Bursaries	$
RESPs	$
Lump Sum from Parents	$
Loan(s)	$
Other:	$
Total Lump-Sum Income	$
LUMP-SUM EXPENSES	
Tuition	$
Books/Supplies	$
Travel to School Start	$
Travel Home End	$
First/Last Rent/Dorm	$
First Grocery Shop/Food Plan	$
Other:	$
Other:	$
Other:	$
Total Lump-Sum Expenses	$
Income – Expenses	$
Less Emergency Fund	$
Monthly Income (What's left ÷ 10 months)	$

Here are the steps to help Darling and Sonny make a plan for how they'll use their lump-sum money:

Step 1: List all the money they'll have from summer employment, scholarships, bursaries, RESPs (the annual lump sum they'll withdraw), gifts from relatives and loans, along with any other money they can scrounge.

Step 2: List the money they know they'll need to cover tuition, books and supplies, travelling to school at the beginning of the year and home again at the end (along with all the trips home in between), first and last months' rent or residence expenses, and the first grocery shop or student food plan.

Step 3: Figure out an amount to set aside for emergencies. DO NOT SKIP THIS STEP. Emergencies happen. That's a part of life. Being financially prepared for them means Darling and Sonny will have options in terms of how they deal with those balls from left field. Being unprepared is immature and short-sighted. I recommend at least $500. Make sure you talk about what constitutes an emergency; not everything is worthy of emergency status, no matter how dramatic Sonny or Darling may be. An emergency is something that threatens your health or ability to continue at school, such as:

• a laptop that suddenly dies (even if it's because someone

poured beer over the keyboard . . . Yes, it really happened to the daughter of a friend of mine)

• a power outage that causes all the food in the fridge to rot (again, yes, it really happened to Alex in her second year at school, when she was living off campus and a tree fell on the power lines)

• a trip home to deal with a sick relative, the death of a family member or friend, or another unexpected family event

Who is in charge of the emergency money? Darling and Sonny need to take responsibility for managing it. You do want them to act like grown-ups, right? Then you must treat them as such. That means if they blow all their "emergency" money on beer and then their laptop dies, you keep your hands out of your pockets.

Step 4: Subtract what needs to be spent from the lump-sum amount and divide the remainder by the number of months at school to give you the amount that will cover monthly expenses. If Darling and Sonny are in a traditional program that lasts eight months of the year (leaving them with four months to work and make money for the next year), they'll have to figure out their budget for eight months. So take whatever is left after the lump-sum calculation and divide it by eight. Some people do school all year round, in which case you'd have to stretch that money over 12 months.

If there's no money left after the lump-sum exercise, work will be a must. There are all sorts of ways for kids to make money or reduce their expenses. Both my editor, Kate, and Alex's BFF, Callie, were residence dons, which meant their room and board were covered. Kids shelve books at libraries, serve coffee and make sandwiches, or work retail. There are some programs that are so intensive that a part-time job isn't an option, in which case maybe Momsie and Pops will pony up with some money to help on a monthly basis.

If there is money left, dividing it up sensibly is the only way to make it last. Regardless, you need to have some sense of where that money is going to go each month.

Once you've helped Sonny and Darling add up what they'll have in a lump sum and what they'll have to lay out in a lump sum (maybe once or twice a year), they will then have to deal with how they'll manage month to month throughout the school year. And here we come to the budget: the plan for how to spend that money in the best possible way.

Rather than using a traditional budget structure, I offer you the "Student Cash-Flow Worksheet" under "Resources" on my site. Again, you can download it and share it with your kids, or you can make your own (there's a sample on pages 76–77).

Student Cash-Flow Worksheet

	Planned	August	Planned	Septembe
Net Income (Total)	$0.00	$0.00	$0.00	$0.00
Income from Work				
Income from Lump-Sum Sources				
Other Income				
IRREGULAR EXPENSES				
Books/Supplies				
Gifts				
Travel				
Medical/Dental				
Insurance				
MONTHLY EXPENSES				
Housing				
Utilities: Electricity				
Utilities: Heat				
Laundry				
Cable/Telephone/Internet				
Cellphone				
Food				
Personal Care				
Car Payments				
Car Maintenance				
Transportation: Gas				
Transportation: Bus/Taxi				
Transportation: Parking				
Clothes				
Entertainment				
Interests/Hobbies/Sports				
Bank Fees				
Taxes				
Debt Repayment				
Emergency Fund				
TOTAL	$0.00	$0.00	$0.00	$0.00
Income – Expenses	$0.00	$0.00	$0.00	$0.00

Bold = essential expense
Italic = non-essential expense

Planned	October	Planned	November	Planned	December	Planned	January
$0.00	$0.00	$0.00	$0.00	$0.00	$0.00	$0.00	$0.00
$0.00	$0.00	$0.00	$0.00	$0.00	$0.00	$0.00	$0.00
$0.00	$0.00	$0.00	$0.00	$0.00	$0.00	$0.00	$0.00

The cash-flow budget is divided into 24 columns, two for each month of the year. The first column for each month is the planned spending for that period; the second is for what actually went out the door. Why so many columns? Well, when you're living so close to the financial line, you need to account for every penny. And since student spending typically varies by month, so should the plan.

I've also coded the actual categories to help Sonny and Darling prioritize. I've found that people have a difficult time telling the difference between WANTS and NEEDS, so I've taken the guesswork out of it. The items in bold type are essential expenses—money that will keep body and soul together. You can spend more or less in a particular category, but you cannot spend more money than you have.

The items in italic type make up less essential needs and wants. You won't die if you can't buy a new winter coat, but it'd sure be nicer than the ratty one you're parading around in now. Ditto cable and a cellphone. Is Internet at home an essential, or can you get by with what's available on campus?

You MUST customize the budget to your circumstances and geographic region. For example, transportation costs may be low if Sonny lives on or near campus (which is why I've put them in italics). But if Darling has chosen to live at home and drive to school, housing costs will be lower and transportation costs higher (and should be in bold because they've become an essential expense), and Darling will also need to budget for things like car maintenance, payments, gas, insurance and the like.

The goal is to spend the least amount so that Darling and Sonny can focus on school instead of work, have some fun and get out without a truckload of debt.

WHAT IS "HELPING"?

Your young adults are on the brink of being independent and solely responsible for themselves. As parents, we want to help them achieve that independence, but we also want to support them in any way we can. But support is not spelled B-A-I-L-O-U-T.

Make sure you and your kids have a solid heart-to-heart about your expectations and theirs before they head off to school, so you are ON THE SAME PAGE.

When my daughter was going to school, I made it clear that she would be responsible for paying a third of her own way through school. I wanted her to have a sense that this education was costing HER something, that it wasn't a free pass. A lot of her friends were surprised to find out that I wasn't picking up the full shot . . . I've got the money.

This was the deal we made:

• Each semester that she carried at least a B+ average would guarantee her the money for the same semester the following year. (This rule did NOT apply to first year because that's a huge transition year and she needed to find her legs.) So if she wanted third-year money, it'd be based on second-year grades.

• Her third was calculated on her total costs, regardless of where the money came from. So both the money from her RESP withdrawals and any money I ponied up for rent were part of the calculation. In essence, we added up all the money she spent that did not come from her own resources (work), and she was responsible for a third of the total.

• While she was ultimately responsible, I agreed to carry her one-third share as an interest-free loan, which she had five years to repay (for an undergrad degree).

That's my way. Not yours. But my question to you is, "Do you have a means by which you will monitor and reward your students?"

No one is ENTITLED to an education. I know it's popular to think we're all entitled to all kinds of stuff . . . but we're NOT. If you want something badly enough, you'll find a way to make it happen. If you don't, all the money thrown at it won't make it a reality.

My daughter was responsible for her own actions. If she chose to take school seriously and work hard, I would support her in any way I could. If she decided to turn a four-year university program into six years of partying, she'd have to find a way to pay for it herself.

Where do you draw the lines? What's important to

you? How far will you go to help your son or daughter? And what will you expect in return?

These are questions you have to answer for yourself. Every child is different. Every parent-child relationship is different. But if you don't lay down the rules of the game from the get-go, that's not fair to anyone. So talk about it with your mate, if you have one. Then talk about it with your son or daughter. Set clear and realistic expectations and then stick to your guns.

SEND THEM OFF WITH SOME LIFE SKILLS

"Clean up your room."

"Get up or you'll be late."

"Empty the dishwasher."

"Why do you leave your crap everywhere?"

"Don't leave your dishes in the sink!"

As parents, we have a round of nagging and ordering that we're used to bellowing at our kids. Let me tell you something: when Alex left home, I did not miss one little bit having her dirty dishes in my kitchen sink. Now she keeps her dirty dishes at her house, and that's fine with me.

I do believe we take for granted what kids "should" know how to do. And it's a far cry from what kids actually can do, because some things just don't occur to them.

Does your kid know how to sew on a button, mend a seam, clean a toilet? How to separate colours for the laundry or how to get out a tough stain? Or how to get that burned-on food off the top of the stove? Do the following statistics surprise you?

- 20% of new university students have never washed their own clothes
- 14% can't boil an egg
- 22% have never shopped for their own food
- 20% have never cleaned a bath or shower
- 69% have never paid a utility bill

As parents, some of us do everything—and I mean EVERYTHING—for our kids. The result is they don't know how to do those things for themselves.

I love to cook, but I've taught both my kids how to cook because I think it's ludicrous that people can't feed themselves lovely meals. The only reason kids live on ramen noodles and cereal while at school is because no one taught them how to stir-fry veggies and make a decent sauce for pasta. Or fry an egg. Or make an omelette.

Can your kids leave a grocery store with good food on their tight budgets? You need to show them how. Take them shopping with you before you send them off to school, show them how you meal-plan and teach them how to check unit prices and find cheaper versions of what they're looking for on top and bottom shelves—or they'll stumble around in the dark for months and rely on ramen noodles and cereal.

Can your kids vacuum, dust, wash floors, scrub bath-tubs and do all the other stuff you do routinely? When are they going to learn?

If you say (in a deep voice), "Oh, they'll learn when they have to do it for themselves," you're missing the point. It's your job as their parent to prepare them for life. And there are important life skills your children should have before you ship 'em off on their own.

Our job, as parents, is to make sure we kick our birdies out of the nest ready to fly. That means having conversations about life, money and responsibilities. It means having expectations of our kids so that they know we know they can manage their lives. And it means allowing the natural consequences to teach important lessons.

If you want your young 'uns to stand half a chance of being empowered and confident adults, don't treat them like babies way beyond the point that they are babies. If you've never had a money talk with your kids right up until the day they're leaving for school, it's still not too late.

Establish some ground rules. Tell Darling and Sonny how much you love them and that you're always there if they want to talk something out. Let them know, however, that it is time for them to take up the reins of their own lives and learn to manage on their own.

Cutting the umbilical cord is often as hard on parents as it is on kids. If you've done your job right, the pain will be minimized. If you're still holding on, rushing in to save the day, helicoptering, it's time to get a life of your own.

They're entitled to theirs.

As Kahlil Gibran wrote in *The Prophet*,

Your children are not your children.
They are the sons and daughters of Life's longing for itself.
. . . .
You are the bows from which your children as living arrows
    are sent forth.